QUITE APART

AKRON SERIES IN POETRY

AKRON SERIES IN POETRY

Mary Biddinger, Editor

Krystal Languell, *Quite Apart*
Brittany Cavallaro, *Unhistorical*
Tyler Mills, *Hawk Parable*
Caryl Pagel, *Twice Told*
Emily Rosko, *Weather Inventions*
Emilia Phillips, *Empty Clip*
Anne Barngrover, *Brazen Creature*
Matthew Guenette, *Vasectomania*
Sandra Simonds, *Further Problems with Pleasure*
Leslie Harrison, *The Book of Endings*
Emilia Phillips, *Groundspeed*
Philip Metres, *Pictures at an Exhibition: A Petersburg Album*
Jennifer Moore, *The Veronica Maneuver*
Brittany Cavallaro, *Girl-King*
Oliver de la Paz, *Post Subject: A Fable*
John Repp, *Fat Jersey Blues*
Emilia Phillips, *Signaletics*
Seth Abramson, *Thievery*
Steve Kistulentz, *Little Black Daydream*
Jason Bredle, *Carnival*
Emily Rosko, *Prop Rockery*
Alison Pelegrin, *Hurricane Party*
Matthew Guenette, *American Busboy*
Joshua Harmon, *Le Spleen de Poughkeepsie*

Titles published since 2010.
For a complete listing of titles published in the series, go to www.uakron.edu/uapress/poetry.

QUITE APART

KRYSTAL LANGUELL

The University of Akron Press
Akron, Ohio

ISBN: 978-1-629221-42-7 (paper)
ISBN: 978-1-629221-43-4 (ePDF)
ISBN: 978-1-629221-44-1 (ePub)

Library of Congress Cataloging-in-Publication Data
Names: Languell, Krystal, 1984– author.
Title: Quite apart / Krystal Languell.
Description: First edition. | Akron, Ohio : The University of Akron Press, 2019. | Series: Akron series in poetry |
Identifiers: LCCN 2018051841 (print) | LCCN 2018055293 (ebook) | ISBN 9781629221434 (ePDF) | ISBN 9781629221441 (ePub) | ISBN 9781629221427 | ISBN 9781629221427(paperback :alk. paper)
Subjects: LCSH: American poetry—21st century.
Classification: LCC PS3612.A5853 (ebook) | LCC PS3612.A5853 A6 2019 (print) | DDC 811/.6—dc23
LC record available at https://lccn.loc.gov/2018051841

∞The paper used in this publication meets the minimum requirements of ANSI/NISO z39.48–1992 (Permanence of Paper).

Cover image: Christine Shan Shan Hou, *Self-actualization (forward movement)*, 7 x 9 inches, collage on paper, © 2018. Used with permission. Cover design by Amy Freels.

Quite Apart was designed and typeset in Mrs. Eaves, with Helvetica Neue display, by Amy Freels and printed on sixty-pound natural and bound by Bookmasters of Ashland, Ohio.

Affordable Learning Initiative
THE UNIVERSITY OF AKRON

Produced in conjunction with the University of Akron Affordable Learning Initiative. More information is available at www.uakron.edu/affordablelearning/

Contents

“first they swear they’ll love you to the grave
next they’re down the woods to dig it for you”
—Denise Riley

“I’m saving up dimes for a rainy day
I got about a dollar laid away”
—Johnny Cash

“I had an interesting experience recently as a woman.”
—Emily Skillings

“I wore your underwear to work the other day
but it didn’t make me feel as sexy as I thought it would.”
—John Yau

Invocation

Poem for My Friend in Philadelphia

By the end of summer, all the decisions
& all the interring, the full shift to open
air will be complete. What it means. You
recall an old dog, muscle past concrete.
The elements conspire, eject their effluvia,
the burst zit of some creature ruins a nice
moment & we put our sunglasses on.
Show me that lighter thing again.

Poem for My Friend in Providence

Do you sometimes feel as if motherhood
is wielded against us? What used to gird me
changed. The big lightbulbs—one, two, three—
foreground honeycomb tiles. I wake up
with a start & nothing is wrong. A field is no
place to panic. The amulet of clarity you gave me:
what am I doing with it? Congratulations
never last. An amethyst at the beach. Your
needle & thread. We can die trying.

Poem for My Friend in Los Angeles

That you've found your name someplace
it doesn't belong, I regret with you.
The scope of gratitude expands so wide
to pre-empt future criticism, inclusive
and ungenerous. And what part
of a list of names is afterthought?
Go alphabetical, camouflage hierarchy.
Didn't you ring people up at Target
for 12 months to get onto a man's margin?
I know you're no feather.

Poem for My Friend in Montreal

Escalator. When carrots still taste sweet,
I know my tongue is clean. It's official.
The paternoster at the Ministry spun
on its chain & I was too afraid to enter
its open compartments. Its beauty—
the frequency with which one can leap
off, cease rising (or descending). A
stomachache at Middlesex Guildhall.
A pause: English lavender with maple
& charcuterie on your terrace. A grief.

Poem for My Friend in Kansas

Are you waiting? The controlled experiment
can fail in spite of its correct plan. Next
time we'll walk the downtown mall slowly.
You'll inherit a lot of diamonds & I will
hang a shadow box displaying scrimshaw.
The gifts travel toward us right now &
you hear yours before you see it. That soft
putter—such a pure stone—is coming closer.

Poem for My Friend in Ohio

I am glad you were not found in a
pit this morning or any other morning
beneath the shed of a troubled white man
in your state. I am glad that we, you and I,
only get groped on the street or
masturbated at on the NJ Transit bus,
that we are alive and not buried and
not buried alive, at least not by dirt,
a shed, that man.

Poem for My Friend in Chicago

Not a pedestal but a kind of chaise
longue of the gut, where love's bile
just wants to relax. We were trying
& I told that creep he got *himself*
thrown out. You can hug this cactus
I got you while your kid is away, if
you feel sad. We wish to half-recline
with our fellow travelers. We gasp
about some chore & either get up
or don't. Settle into a relational
aesthetic: experiential Pyrex & velvet.
I'd take an elective course on that.

Poem for My Friend in Brooklyn

Feeling very named, you hesitate
to condemn a man. Your star quality
directs you to keep an open heart
even as you sometimes suffer
loneliness in your hub. You mean
to complete & to hum. The aphorisms
broadcast: *feel free*. A new moon brings us
success, dampened by private crumbling.

Poem for My Friend in Maine

To agree, we say, "Correctol 44,"
an anti-diarrheal that's been taken off
the market. To scold, we say, "Very poor!"
At Olive Garden my language got stuck
& I ticced. The rabbits we liberated from
your father lived a number of years. I found
your letters from Spooner, but I didn't open
them because almost nothing is worth
reliving, certainly not your first banishment.
Tucked in with postcards my mother sent
from the Mayo Clinic. This must be another
woman's life: wild greens & Icelandic yogurt
by the jar, the trucker barreling toward Acadia.

Poem for My Friend in Virginia

I heard a marching band over the mountain
& you heard it too & later on the road I cried
at a rainbow. You tell me how to deal with
my bleeding when it surpasses me. Together
at the party, we took a ceremonial silver platter
home in our tote bag to glamorize our relation.
The tyrant spoke: *This can't turn into an experiment.*
We are still working to heat it hot enough to melt.

Last Song

A door slams, and I want to push someone into a swimming pool.
The summers it does nothing but rain, we have bad hair.
A man I admire says yes to invitations with enthusiasm. We
are not the helpless kind of person, my friend the addict says.
Then he disappears. Holding out a palm to feel for raindrops,
when your whole body is the palm. A funeral stops the calendar
like a funeral, a free pass to absent yourself. Tiny pillow,
embroidered, is the small cushion her millions offer her.

I drove to the cemetery moon on Strawberry Road, giving rides.
I kept hoping to dream about getting fucked. I was very alone.
What's behind the diamond is skin, earnestly, the big organ.
Kids don't touch feathers because birds have germs. I peel apart
the good and bad. The man with a long book on water is eager
to explain how a flood is sad. He gave up his accent. A ragged
state visit where you tell what you did to deserve detention.
An ant's crawling on me and I wake up from my nap.

It's okay if killing an insect gives you a little pleasure.
Staticking out my hearing to generate a conversation starter.
I'm curled up on my mountain I paid a lot of credit for,
sitting still in a hard chair like a woman doing as she's told.
Washout the landscaping, take me out of the spiral. Rain comes
and after plain causeway, a minor mistake, I nearly confess to fraud.
Flask, flash, rumble: all in need of a new form of engagement.
He won't leave the farm. My friend's next-door neighbor was gutted.

What a nice girl feels is nothing but solutions.
The stock market turns on opiates, not purity.
A typical problem takes the young girl out. Her parents
invest in the hospital for her lucky breakdown.
She pleads and he says, “you’re nice,” then she’s carried off.
More of border patrol’s surveillance blimps appear, tethered.
Saved from ruin, she throws her body around in recovery.
Poor and rural women always take the brunt of regulation.

Tonight this is our last song, he said, then played a few more.
You'd cast the steel of my ring in wax, paying me attention,
which turned out flat, making another useless gesture.
The song was my necessary hiding place. It had to be long.
About whether two years or one has passed, the cheater feels unsure.
He says, "Amen," and the women say, "No." He repeats it, undeterred.
My ceiling leaks, my car is packed. You've got a good heart, I heard.
I'm instructed to pop bubbles in the lead-based paint. What a risky fuel.

Relax into receiving benefits or refuse entrapment by the cops
parked outside the bar. A neutral man keeps a list of their strategies.
The commissioner sends an email; he advises that laptops have been
a hot item for theft since their invention. Jagged cut in half, and
half my heart is under a hood. The rest yells through the wall
like a bad husband. We let our hot items out of our sight.
He only hosted the parties, but still he was liable. I can be a snob
about the law when the law is clear. My gray hairs look blonde.

Closely watch your best move, the naming. Double stop.
That is, two ideas at once in music. Hold the pair of them.
I wanted to be two in all ways, and one other said I had failed.
Him, he married a woman with the same name as his mom.
My talent voided, love all wrong. I felt like a child, not
wifely. Accepting the role means agreeing to be harmless.
The Queen of Swords has an evil twin. Once she detached
from the king, a flower grew under the throne, became a hinge.

Whatever you said in your bedroom voice, I eavesdropped on
the tone. Maybe I shoplifted as a child. In the drugstore,
toys followed me home, made notes on a little spiral pad about
the trouble to come. Driving through mountains, edges rear up,
deep concern manifests as a veer to stay in my lane. A psychic
said I'll get what I want, but that wasn't the question I asked.
We lived in close quarters and were absolutely no use to each other.
With no boost, what can we do against a total lack of moorage.

Every first day of school, you might be the new girl.
If you were a poor kid, what was the feeling of wanting.
Now I can spend the old anxiety on nice food, milk
in a glass jar I reuse. Forgiveness operates subtly.
A man at a holiday party asked me what I do.
I wasn't able to give a clear report, so he filled in
the diminutive. The truth is, I'm doing dangerous work
prematurely, sweating in my greenhouse so I can eat.

Forgetful in confinement, in the sun I get alert
so I don't run my neighbors over. Through a cloud
we get on the big bridge, and I pretend for the little girl.
We get very quiet while I enter the blizzard steering zone,
concentrating like Johnny O who looks up, looks
down to see a flag here in the snow. As long as I can,
I line up to red taillights, then lose ground to slippage.
Show me how you stay calm, crawling with the best effort.

Which male mythology do I choose: Wolf River
or Victoria? He knows he has an effect on certain women,
and he'll use it against me. In my idle gossip, I take
a for-instance to its extreme, conjuring a surprise death
narrative. You can practice the move or sidestep it instead
of tumbling in like I do. Trained by a radical girlhood,
I resented learning to pretend to be uncertain.
"Keep safe," the men say. "You'd better take that energy home."

I won't ask whether you remember my quarts of frozen milk
in the freezer. I was creatively bored, broke, culinary. The ristra
man sold rotting vegetables across the street, and his cat
lying around swatted its tail. The cat enjoyed a life of its own.
A man, a hyper-empath, sat down at the table with a half-formed
complaint. Injustice was the subtext, so I became interested, ready
to react, but a philosopher said, "Let's drop it." I take some pleasure
in upset. He went on to describe the band as spooky in their capes.

If I tell you to sex up the deadbolt, can you feel it out?
Turn the key but don't force it. That's good advice generally,
even in two equally acceptable scenarios. One led to a
handsome husband, her ticket out of here. Value judgment
ranked the second a poverty too low, in her view, then
he drove me in his big car to the burnt-out condo showing
off his savvy, he the unspeakable criminal. As he practiced
his speech, as limit made a poison, she slipped into habit.

To survive the murder plot you stumble into: when you're
injured, say you were with friends. We were playing
in the alley, barefoot and peeping in garage windows.
I cleaned the blood off my yellow bike horn later. Nobody
came looking for me. I had a neighbor's rhubarb pie.
Often I mimic, now that I'm not a child. A friend said
I pronounced my mentor's name wrong, and I said I'd try
to improve. A scar on my heel reminds me of class shame.

What do you do when you're not getting stressed out?
I code an idea, then wonder at the severed connection
between body type and psychoanalysis for the girl
twirling her baton. Glory makes a cameo in the plot.
A new season arrives in which we hope to do less harm.
Lots of people have bad teachers. Forgettable is fine.
For lyrical feeling, drop a Euro coin in the fountain and hum.
A stranger comes to town and becomes your boyfriend.

Middlemarch Poems

June 10

the study of a character
where individual ethic surfaces
it's the unaccustomed depth where fervor
is lived
it's solitude in imagination
planning the perfect crime but
never intending to actually do it
the unclarity of lacking a boss to please
with any love gesture of pure work

be love in every word
the mantra extracted from careful observation
constant non-performance
did Aristotle say something
about trying repeatedly even overcompensating
for known inadequacies
or was that a less ancient
that idea relies on binaries of good & evil
anyway
does the slippage fall back down into hate then
if ideas are basic seesaw simple machine combo
a wedge and a lever
a tool

say yes to requests
for favors or borrowing
share with anybody
without judgment
unless
as is sometimes the case

the truth tells itself and is not pretty
is someone else falling short of
being love manifest

motto not mantra
channeling energy
to a person in need of invisible
support against an obstacle
it is vague and it will continue
on the same path of not your business
as long as your mind is closed
to magic
if you want to be a witch
you must relent
abandon the reflex that first sight
tells you anything true at all

June 11

going about a quickly
invented errand to improve
his chances
a man may make an error
in judgment with no friend
witnessing against hasty
horse trading
you know men will trade
horses as long as there are horses
still around
trotting or cantering
having speculative value

the imagination left
to itself is drunk on perfume
is in gridlock traffic
so owing an apology
is a special pain

what crow
what defeat is this
a bulky pack
no end to unpleasant surprise
must reorient the rogue mind
off thinking its own important
thoughts
all full with rectitude
wonderland of
obstacles
what C.S. Lewis had to say

about salt
how if you told an alien
we put it on everything
they'd be repulsed
at our lack of sense

June 12

the glances at rival brocade
belie the seriousness of bringing
a matter to one's attention
which unchecked may further
limit one's future happiness

to an individual with a single purpose
what else can come to mind
her own flirtation bloats
and what explodes or what relents
in response to her waggle of fingertips
true the setting is provincial but
the families don't feel small to
themselves or their bank president
impulse toward gain
softening of ideology
a few teardrops fall and it's decided
wake up on time and practice a hobby
a drama of manners where no one
is rude quite apart from differing opinion
factions exist but tempers are mild
men's health however enters unclarity
he must not be made anxious in the
slightest a task put to a girl to enforce
who has weighty anxieties already that
must now become secret and how will
keeping secrets suit her
charge of protection
to keep watch of a strange stuffy man
she'll keep the task
and the men's sensitivities will all outgrow

a certain couch in a certain room
with dust motes in what light gets in
full of unread books she'll curse the full
contents of the house before long
to an eye dead to collars and ornament
a heart wanting a worthy of depth

June 15

give the mourners ham and veal
while the master lies in his bedrest
men seated in the kitchen with their
googly eyes on the girl keeping them
fed on master's pantry
waiting for the fatal blow
blood entitles the guests to dine on
whatever stores the property contains
and the young layabout also ill and
the aged scholar husband also ill
gloom persists
he states he has made his will
and swipes with his gold-handled
cane at the intruders
has a man a right to swing at his blood
undocumented how he acquired property
yet depth of detail on ethic of girl
preparing death feasts for cousins et cetera
asks the wrong mother for advice
nature of provinciality
word is deed and only so few chances
the doctor considered kind of a laborer
not as desirable as thc big landowners for
marriage material
provincial overlaps much with superrich
in cities too just fewer books and worse cut
of trousers or jib

June 16

about the engagement
the father says the doctor is
a poor man
the doctor buys a dinner service
it's quite expensive
but he thinks since you only buy it
once & does not consult his
dear in this domestic task
so eager to rush the wedding to
get through it men keep imagining
that marriage will calm her
& then they can get back to work
science or philosophy research with
the benefit of the limit to womanly
education just enough to keep busy
in the house ready with affection &
music at any moment in short trained
for servitude without selfhood as if
this matched the girl each engaged himself
to but maybe they think opinions solely
come for wedding party details and a bit
the honeymoon itinerary what's the big
deal he thinks a bunch of nonsense yet
the order of things is resultant and its
inverse you see completely reliant on
family mores of an ethic the boy's gone
quite pale as he'd made plans to do nothing
the timeline is set by tradition and rut
comes from wear which is confirmation
that one who wishes to alter the course finds
himself alone in the tall grass of a moment

June 17

the time for her ideas was on the
matter of wallpaper and linens
she asks permission to speak
is often told that's the last of it
to build safe cottages or advise
on what's fair and righteous better
suits her but now the man's health
is brought in for a reason to value
his thoughts as superior spare him
the stress of disagreement
the type that won't notice her loss
of vim appreciate the silence
accompanying her while she is serious
no music or ornament as with most
women she wants to read and be
of use to the world what opportunities
does he imagine he affords her
how long must she be grateful for
her boring honeymoon spent touring
art and architecture site after site
how fortunate that she be young and
formidably unsilly yet before long he'll
wish he had a stupid bride or none at all
instead of this unusual figure
gritting her teeth minding her inner life

June 18

the scholar determines who is welcome
visitor to his landholdings and table
lets his mood flip in the face of non-ideal
news imagines himself a kind of king
on what grounds must he be obeyed is it
the purity of his blood aristocratic destiny
doesn't want a cousin so far below him
it offends him deeply to what end must
a record of his injured feelings be kept
he is rich it's confirmed and all his tenants
live in safe comfortable cottages with no
squalor whatsoever sometimes the thought
of women married to rich old men is enough
to cry about a perfect squalor of inner life
what depth is possible when all is either whisper
or palliative nursing so the job is to wait for
his death which is a mean small hope pray
you don't die in childbirth before you can enjoy
what he's left you unless he too is a secretive
petty old crank who wishes to see you faint
at his coffin when you learn you'll be going to
stay with uncle somebody he gets the last laugh
that's how this has always worked

June 20

good news inspires the big flawed heart
to make plans for sharing income prior
to official agreement contract
if terms shift out of speculation into say
an unpaid internship wife unit
will bop his nose certainly while
daughter who was called an old brick
by a child would be redisappointed too
trust of a good letter come by post
what of the other seven letters for father
that day a noon meeting proposed
did he remember to send his reply or
was the idea misfiled into a drafts folder
in new workplaces too we make mistakes
wonder what will these people think
it's nervous to see others flinging trust
around as if it were infinite and ready
what if we only have a little what if we
go hungry for it later and wish differently

June 21

shifted into a different house
and then a new set of concerns
it was just yesterday
the husband asked the doctor
what was really wrong with him
the husband is very distrustful
suspects his wife of wrong motives
the journalist nephew of designs
on the wife seems to be cooking up
some adjustments to his will
as predicted in these pages
few characters in the plot in pursuit
of doing good for humankind
not so much aware that such a
phenomenon exists just a self and
a few acquaintances a few officials
that lucky dad who has been at work
for causes and not pay wants to help
the layabout rich boy but really should
keep his attention on his own several
children he is the big
heart in town who gives it all away mister
set a little imaginary income aside
nonetheless

June 28

on the topic of medical advice
blistering is a common treatment
when physicking falls short
the pills a fertile mother takes to
get through a busy month of baking
the brown rather than pink recipe
has worked for years a tumor they
might want cut but first it's manners
among doctors offense his patient
cured better by a younger man better
because the servant was no longer sick
and with no cutting into her others
from the brink of death some say
unnaturally no autopsy practice in
place the young doctor thinks aloud
of graverobbing historical figures
to his wife's disgust who says no
misery please for us make discoveries
without upsetting people they have
a little consumer debt having rushed
the wedding the banker built the new
hospital though a low profession
other bodies' fluids and temperaments
says wife she is opposed to muck & bile

June 30

a second time a young woman refuses
to obey a man and he's dead by morning
'by' in this case stretches to include the
period of hours prior to his expiration
slumped over a picnic table in his cape
frantic work and the next chapter
skips ahead weeks a woman in grief
what does she do how is it different than
sitting in her room with a few books
and a window would be hard to notice
his absence no one passing her a note
about what room to eat her dinner in
next marker will be the day to open
his desk someone interprets the will at
her its codicil appended to exert control
from the grave who'll never receive a
portion of the wealth the only person
she had spoken up for to split the land

July 3

romance came about during illness
in the mayor's house anyone left
unsupervised might fall in love
the unmarried meet each other
then forget their oaths to self one
bride had a boy baby the doctor's
wife miscarried horseback riding
knocked her fetus loose still he
could not be angry with her now
she has sneaked that they might
not sell the house to her ex-suitor
and she not admitting simply
her humiliation instead she meddles
in business unlike her unlike a lady
to begin a foray into meeting agents
provincial how she writes to relatives
thinks only of the men's opinion of her
appearance not considering the ladies
might not want her around much
plaits a nuisance vanity can be called
another name depends on the context
surface or aesthetics labor is another
the mayor's pretty daughter thinks men
will invite her to live on family land
she wishes they would move to London

July 7

after she said she wished she'd died
with the baby mister doctor went to
the gambling house to see a man about
some business and began betting at cards
and winning for a time but embarrassing
himself when spendthrift brother-in-law
arrived himself a bit in shame a man of
pleasures and called him away to another
meeting he could compose himself shake
off the spell brother gets a warm advice but
doctor is alone in his affairs might be that
bank president will ask him to do away with
the alcoholic troublemaker now holed up
on his property there would be some
money in that for him while banker yet
worries himself ill considers moving his wife to
the next town over to hide wealth got from others'
losses making loans and pawning for the desperate
predatory indeed he absorbed the widow's holdings
on her death even as he knew her daughter was
living he sensing the end would do well to indulge
a loan to the poor doctor seeing how stress of
protecting his wealth is killing him is it habit that
prevents his generosity he says his wife's family has
borrowed large sums of his it is their extravagant
educations that accustom them to a life failing to
also acquire skills or business to afford their tastes
are quite outside their budget yet they cast about for
reasons would the boy have earned like they hoped in
the clergy as he would find need of for his own family

July 11

not much going right anymore
villain dispatched victim fancies
himself passive though he's arranged
the man's expiration aggressively
while no one of consequence looked
on the respite brief since rascal'd
already told the secret all over as he
was a drunk and one cannot trust
a drunk to silence gave the opium and
the brandy and covered it up opposing
medical views provide alibi one man
knew and it was known but did he plan
to kill him his land agent as well novels
make plain evil once indulged doesn't
relent in its appeal consequences expose
the wrongdoing only inasmuch as it
cannot go on replicating itself without
incurring severe punishment or why
check power banker is elderly popular
opinion was against him anyway but
now it's turned out of hand his heart
cannot cycle his breath in regular puffs
collapse at town meeting melodrama
but at seventy perhaps the man just dies

July 15

no one else died and the kids got
married like they wanted to after
finally admitting they felt love in
each other's company all only once
she set aside her misery having slept
on the floor in her gown sobbing
returned to her rival to still set right
the matter of debts and rumors which
seemed to her total injustice she spoke
for the doctor volunteered to meddle
in repair to his reputation as an honest
man and true even her solutions work
every time they benefit others such was
her religion in practical terms despite
her perception that her own lover held
this wife's hands to his mouth and pulled
away in shame when she entered letter in
her hand to explain how she'd fix some
element of their ruin dropped the letter on
the desk and walked out to sob at home
all her interest faded away and yet plot had
her return to finish her favor and unfold
of consequences led to epilogue marriage
she did give up all the land to be with him
the formerly idle painter the spurned heir

Lost Song

You admit you prefer monied friends and I realize
you are a rich person. Essentially, yes, that's the glass
ceiling in New York. Your vanity climbs a weird ladder.
I am still myself. Critical. Imagine self-education—loving
the force of a wave until it reminds you you are weakness.
A rocket pinpricks the Earth's atmosphere as a body
quakes the floor, rattles one particular glass in the cabinet,
storming out. Ta-da! Without wealth you are vapor.

Full thunder. Confess I got on the highway prematurely.
I noticed a bruise on my tattoo and thought it was rubbing off.
When I remember death, I'm unimpressed with my output.
And then, do you consider your life easy? On moon day,
the chef said he adds his own minerals to water. Drop
the dead sparkler in the empty tequila bottle as a precaution.
Wrap it up in tissue paper. Send it down the escalator.
A scholar of girlhood didn't know our jump rope rhyme.

O identifiers, a girl on the fringe gets reduced to a fraction
in foggy glass. By not replacing clothes in tatters, I save
on expenses while getting jealous of crowds, tourists even
with their new sneakers. Heat makes her sing the alphabet
to gauge exhaustion. Basking in the city, what else is there
to do but shock people, enter a gallery space poorly attired.
O signifieds, the thing itself. The rotting shoe in the Danube.
He notices I'm a good sleeper. I never thought about it.

Mannequins go in a big museum of artifacts, confirming
the history of civilization is repeated gossip about cliques.
The group said I looked like a new woman and then moved
away as one, barking, "Couture's not dead!" They built a monument
to their nostalgia disguised as critique of fast fashion. That was
the week no one shopped out of respect for garment factory
worker deaths. Alone, I walked through the exhibit twice. Black
plastic bunting overhead. Its flaws were as stunning as promised.

When it's a miracle to be here, does my gratitude need
to be my red carpet? People keep telling me I don't have to
work alone, but after my accomplice turned tail, my loot
disappeared with him. Imagine a decade of clenched teeth
despite the sudden freedom to marry up and earn peace.
I command and code-switch into my stretch mark, a common
gesture in my spiritual life. What do you know about how I work?
That ethic doesn't grant partial credit to the obstacle in its way.

She calls me her fiendish reminder of incomplete work.
People check her glands, she swallows hard. A fresh paint job
chipped at by bug guts. The side effect damages mothers who
are afraid of not doing enough, who hit their kids on the subway
first one slam then regress to a few years ago. Down the hall
with the same righteous formula, she dragged a thick fabric
cover at an odd hour. Worse, overactive germs get in the nailbed.
I say I'm coming to take care of it. A way out of ability's ache.

Outside, a kid teaches himself the bridal march on a keyboard.
I tried the same thing and a rash bloomed up my throat.
Were we telling secrets? The king died and made me king.
He called what I'd been enjoying "spa music." I reached over
like when I almost put my gentle voice in your hand. Go
ahead to the corner to cop in bright colors beneath the tower.
Certain cult activities have become less popular. Cold water snaps
me back—a timeline was central, but for others it's secondary.

Infused with anger, my heart pumps hard. I bear it around.
Noticing, I buy a loosie for a teenager. Some unseen
negative thing happens, and then everyone turns left.
A woman stuffs her child into the backseat of a car.
Quick up the street police the wrong way up. No blood.
Cops running toward a noise. And I will be extraneous.
When he gets out of jail, he bleaches the hall. Passing by,
father figure makes the shape of a gun with his hand.

We are the diagram. And you're in the spirit too.
Walking conversation on trash cans and new mayor.
Doing very good now with your greeting, instigator.
The tyrant called my mother to say I'd been bad so
she'd banish me to the desert. A battery, a spider:
proximate stuff inside your space and out. Afraid of
the factual background, I was in it for the acoustics.
That unhappy threat needs me. Too early, bullets flew.

Affordable resort town, some local people's seasonal
second and third jobs tending bar with a staph infection.
In the past, someone I trust says she can see I am sad.
Now the time has passed. To report on him, the cost.
Allium or zinnia, she prefers either to violets in a fist.
Neighbor says she chooses not to vote, avoiding jury duty.
Neighbor says get a rubber heel. Our control ruthless.
Call it addiction to lockdown; pop, lock and drop it.

I drank a bottle of Perrier before bed and dreamed that
Nick Cave was begging to fuck me. In the dream, I said no.
I said there is a time and a place. Then I started drinking Perrier
before bed every night to bring him back. It never works.
Don't suppose what a song will do for your sex channel.
Alertness cost. Because I do harvest the idea of a hunkering.
A woman yells the word quiet. Flies hatched in my window
frames. A germ has no gender. She's a germ. A dandelion.

In the would-you-rather, I chose chewing broken glass. Lead paint frightens me less than decades of fiberglass in fingertips and lungs, which remains matchless for poison. She said kids don't want to work, as if that made them bad thinkers.
What has work ever done for her? She survives. The glassy wool routes into her membranes. On the difference between ongoing swagger and unfragility, woman remarks. She is only on stage to open a door. She, bereft in the dark with a half-soul.

Threw the shirt down. Shirty. I'm drunk on two beers like
a girlfriend can be. Our window, cracked, spiderwebs out and out
unrepaired. Boyfriends always bring speakers to my apartment.
Not much of a sad part to Graceland, despite the graves and basic facts.
Where I'm from, members of the public tour the Studebaker ruins.
Most notable now for its closure. Broken things pass for news, delusion
about staying broken. Broken whiteness as much a myth as any war.
The best part of a year on the highway was forgetting the assembly line.

It is Christmas, and it is also Wednesday. Just a bit short.
Easier last time. Always waiting for business hours to start.
Left all his sentimental things in a hotel room. Praise with force.
Tried to gather. Making a real effort to keep back from abyss.
Still, drank a latte I didn't need for the transition value from
one labor to the next, before the third shower. Confirm receipt.
The impending untenable. Yawn at the canvas of simultaneity.
I go to the store and tell my problem to a fellow customer.

Makes a pocket flip and a crease tuck after belt bounce.
They talk real estate. In sweatpants thinking about money.
Where is she welcome. If they say she gently reifies on spec.
Heels collapse forward in a slow slam and big flip of tails.
They billow. Can she tell the mutual problem without worsening.
Got an excuse for everything. Scrap can be made useful.
Dynasty question mark. Heard he was a real pill. A period.
End the program of disillusionment. Usher in the grande dames.

Little Runaway

(I had a system) (it worked)

(I did not then have New York City)

(I did not have (a net-work) (city cousin) (inheritance) (savvy))

(I stapled) (could learn by working)

(long arm stapler) (copied Adobe Suite in the back of mentor's van)

(a folder with pouch of disks)

(I am no astronaut looking back at the globe) (am planet-life)

(ultimate earthrise) (very much planted, stationary)

(other systems w/ code and formula) (mine: exhaustive / vertical)

(I am no astrolabe) (or astrocyte) (glue cell)

(then came time)

(My sister was this) (she worked)

        (She did not then have spirit gear)

(She did not have (property of) (points) (bonus / combat pay))

        (She worked in bulk) (she still does)

(My system) (lacked) (style)

        (it was bulk) (memory says (twenty) (in a list) (a mile))

(fight the mill)   (the job) (jog on tread)   (pestle metaphor)

        (My apology) (for (space) for (wind))   (the long walk I took)

(the arroyo (yes) (I followed the arroyo)) (and my guts) (mutinied)

        (My sister (she) drives on the ice) (without difficulty)

(and (here) (comes) (climate))   (to place) (your life) (in context)

(The policy was private)   (after all)

    (five x five x five (sometimes four)) (foraging postage)

(I didn't think)   (I swam alone)   (kept secrets)

    (Automated how I live)   (not established (with trim))

(Besides)   (in the library basement) (mispronouncing) (attn morale)

(was another inch (routine))   (crates drip (meltdown) from cold storage)

        (Congressional Record)

(for a few dollars)   (Later) (later) (the bulldozer) (as usual)

    (Later the policy) (became matter)   (coursing)

((a note) (a dial) (a photo) left inside the screen door)   (Pause)

        (to set aside)   (your work (only scalar quantity))

(It did not (account)) ((frantic nature) into (common surprise))

(A goal to be everywhere) (live a life in every house along the highway)

(Its vast imaginary) (What about after survival)

(What about (other) (twists) (other funded) (her agenda))

(The business of) (double agency (It preferred neutral) (when the nest) (burned))

(I would) (keep (at) (the))

(keep on about) (a little sporting) (a whistling tune)

(What its own self (a priori) (dictated) was host (needs to depart))

(It (the game of prizes) having cash in sight) (What prestige in gaze (on) looking)

(Her victory (having oversold the pitch))

(The business of (business I've mentioned before)) (and my bills) (and mortality)

(A license (for these brothers to be my brothers)) (if I want)

(It was (pointedly) true how (the denial was depression) what I want) (is warmth)

(Non-young) (My slang (is idiomatic))

(The business of years (and of hedging a future)) (It becomes urgent)

(In her case tax advantage) (It would roll over) (It would (penalty))

((If) I adhere) (all agents assemble) (the holidays swept)

(Recall scant celebration) (Y2K in the car (a rainy night)) (the loss of it)

(allow me (to interject)) (What about shoulder (separation))

((you splinter) (my interest) (in)) ((anew) (I am) outside) (I am (for one) (other))

(The work (simple)) (The bullshit (simple)) (Limited natural talent (or endurance))

(Chain of tasks (some of us help each other) (some of us are liars))

(Way to the future (loose grasp) (transparency)) (ideas without incentive)

(How to put the charge (into) (powered objects)) (let the thing see you (foam))

(Know what else (maybe anciently) prefigured this pool)

((A pebble) in the gullet) (a sour cancer) (the (American) pastime)

(Are you sure) (No (never)) (But I know you (you're the same guy))

(White gangsters wear ties (in the white imagination))

(Compulsory (otherwise (lacking insurance) over fifty (body wrecked)) service)

(Then unsatisfied) (You still have not heard me)

(Bringing into compliance (with all this planning)) (Audience says they are tired)

(Message or management) (The choir says (metaphor is not plastic))

(Set up as a game (theory) to matter) (Open door (not a free entry) step right adjacent to it)

(A long day) (Sticky problem (larceny's damage) (which witch))

(A hard year) (The key) (Oh (my love's gift too (chooses)))

((The star) (is asking a lot again) pat me down right (swat) (prep) (I can))

(Take it like a (what are you supposed to be)) (an available feature (at a cost))

(Upsetting) ((I mean) moment-by-moment choice) (Can I flourish)

(Harvest) (Temperature and mood (shaky hands))

(Unromantic (dropped bowl (shattered (bounced back in my face))))
(Step away)

(Smell of (bonfire) smoke in my sweater (in class learning (to close accounts)))

(The last fire) (What year was it) (What state was I in)

(a trash fire) (unsafe to inhale (paperwork) (treated wood) (valentines))

(A clever word) ((stretches to clamor) (stretches to joy) (to noisy family))

((Primary) (chaos) dogs of hell) (Simply raising questions)

(Boredom makes a program)

(Doing the wash) (Doing the fold (am saintly)) (indexical (weak))

(Here is a positive message) (laughing together) (Happy to see excellence)

(And cool is comfort (in the flex of expertise))

((Certain) (unsurprised at the stuff)) (plans of the world (we all go as one))

(She loves her (grief))   (a reward (for sitting through meetings))

(My people (get into jams) (teeth knocked out) (fleshy tissue))

(She says (don't tell him that))   (The men have no jobs)

(The women do)   (Apartments (like trailers) were for poor people (back there))

(She said (it doesn't make sense) (what do you (get)) (to not know anyone))

(Rote memorization)   (Thinking I would do (but a woman said I was a myth))

(Combative on occasion)   (Turning (so negative) (I) (told) (you))

((Into) (emergency fund (where I come in)))

(Take note) (reverse card (carrying too many swords))

((Removing myself from the situation)   (harmed no one)) (I said to myself (soft))

(The system slept)   (The city rose up)

(Factories closed for the holidays (a shutdown) (machine stoppage))

(I had an opportunity (cost-benefit) which I took
(begrudging the limit to it))

(The limit on my life expectancy (by county))

(I want to make clear) (You will outlive me (it's regional) (industrial))

(And most of the time (I know I am no moon-man (moon-god)) (I
accept))

(This is the middle already (of my life))   (Back home)

(Perversity at the biker bar)   (five dollar (meat on bread))
(Our parents)

((lost their keys ((in the snow)) (in the parking lot) (late)))

(addiction has my uncle eating off the floor) (And my work is to discuss)

(I will take you apart) (Him he just drops in (and talks))

(He says (blood) and (pig) and (bride) (fucker) (satan) (me))

(and they (read it)) (and his want is a problem)

(A note on my desk says (call it a fellowship)) (take heart)

(Surplus leaves are racking up outside)

((I can say all the same vulgar things) (plus not answer my phone))

(He turns in a list) (he reveres the act) (these guys know who to ask)

(How relieving ((not at all)) not being a target) (I only got
played)

(Challenges the stare with ((can I help you)) (you keep looking over here))

(I ask) (Do you have some kind of problem) (Keeping scrap to
incite)

(A neighbor stopped me (I was passing her store) (I was generally
disgusted))

(She gestured to the street) (and said (You can't take all of
this in))

((Make your mind like a piece of glass))

(I feel a deep moral debt) (a suspicion towards joy)

(At the farmers market) (my desire so appropriate)
(I allow myself to feel it)

(pure (abundance) of choice) (a mouth full of luxury tomato with
salt)

(Talking to death) (advancing and clutching
at)

(a stalk of Brussels sprouts (in conversation with) (sauerkraut
in a jar))

((Here) food is cheap when raw (tonics for health))
(lavender sachets)

(The woman gave me licorice incense) (she said) (try this)

(Nerve damage)   (Upstairs behind a window (looking down))

(with fellow feeling)

(averse to secrets) (much of the work) (under
nondisclosure)

(bound to earth) ((to endure) body pain)   (what of revenge)

(Their bad faith is necessary) (crisis of the small heart)

(connotation of a pledge)   (curled toes over time
(possibly inevitable))

(repulsion plus malfunction)   (witness how (who) she takes care)

(her juice) (all over) (that big lashed eye)

(says we buoy our own) (a strain) (a query)   (choosing who to cut)

(clashing)   (in favor) (to rest) (send money) (as proof)

(We begin with (an invocation)) (Affiliating with the right god)

((Is respect no more) (than self-defense))

(The diction implies) (you should know (the reference))

(After means since when do I care)

(Once it's way too late to place blame)

(Only I was encouraged to respond) (to) (neighborhood
politicking)

(When I had returned from) (mosquitos and sawdust) (in
the piss trough)

(In light (of recent events)) (all balconies rebolted)

(We signal emergency) (crash into a berm) (pointless)
(without a witness)

(Where did my needle go) (tucked in an envelope)

(I might listen for)   (how untried this girl is)

(Keeping scrap in sight (case of reeds) (useful things))   (trained pose
too)

(Listen)   (if the way it works is (smile and turn into
expensive stone))

((Routine) the slow way family sloughs off)

(The idea is chemical harvested from (doubts))

(Another time) (Through-line of mockery)   ((in the effort) to be kind)

(Clearly no body at the center)   (an arena of seasonal products)

(State the obvious (misapprehension))   (it happens to lots of people)

(Which way from here)   (loud conditions)
(muscles tear)

(Yet recall the full range of lives)   (You've thought wrong many
times)

(The essay on modesty) (in application for) (bodily autonomy)

(She lost that case) (on (wide is the gate)) (rhetorically
memorable)

(Arbiter rise)

(Attracted to) (the most minor) (advantages) (adopting gendered
props)

(Assaying willingness) (I notice a certain scarlet
letter)

(Dream of a house) (it can't be mine) (vast roominess)

(Dream of a beach) (but it's a beach with a problem)

(In the smug of your (natural woman)) (I have had (a stain)
(a conceit))

(Despite appearances (allegedly))

(A medical person) (declares the injury a non-emergency)

(the passports curled up) (it was so humid in our rented room)

(travel to forget the criminal element) (in my bad blood)

(Nothing very significant at the cemetery) (an unremarkable lunch
salad)

(The thrift shop closed six months ago)

((We lit candles for a man who died) (rusted cellar grate)) (near to home)

(I was afraid (and I made my friend afraid too))

(another woman altogether said they may be
(murderers))

((I'm more worried about) being backed over by construction vehicles)

(in other places) (I do pray for my family's safety)

(mother says it isn't working)

(She drove me to the airport) ((and she said))

(she said) (she said) (She said)

(she said) ((she said))

(she said) (she said)

(We pulled up) (for me to take a bus) (to a bigger airport)

(she said) (Your cousin wanted to see you—)

((she said))

(—but I wouldn't let him)

(She said she wouldn't) (give him my phone number)

(I saw him newly-born) (and in his car seat) (a boy)

Notes

"What a nice girl feels is nothing but solutions" is based on *Splendor in the Grass* (1961), which I watched as research for reviewing Karen Rigby's book *Chinoiserie* (Ahsahta Press, 2012).

"Mannequins go in a big museum of artifacts, confirming" responds to the "PUNK: Chaos to Couture" show at MoMA in 2013. In his *New Yorker* review (May 7, 2013), "The Day Punk Died Again," Sasha Frere-Jones issues one of the most punishing dismissals of the twenty-first century: "There is no axis along which this exhibit functions properly: the historical, anecdotal, or superficial."

The music referred to throughout is most often Nick Cave, Jeff Buckley, or Jason Molina.

Acknowledgments

Many of these poems have appeared in the following publications: *A Dozen Nothing*, *American Poetry Review*, *Bayou Magazine*, *Bennington Review*, *BOAAT*, *Boog City*, *Boston Review*, *Colorado Review*, *EK*PHRA*SIS*, *Entropy*, *The Felt*, *Fence*, *Fourteen Hills*, *Glass: a Journal of Poetry*, the Academy of American Poets' *Poem-a-Day*, *The Poetry Project Newsletter*, *Prelude*, *Tract/Trace*, and in the anthology *Ritual and Capital* published by Wendy's Subway and the Bard Graduate Center.

"*Middlemarch* Poems" appeared as an online chapbook called *The Big Flawed Heart*, published by Essay Press in 2017.

Some poems from "Last Song" and "Lost Song" appeared in the chapbook *Last Song*, published by dancing girl press in 2014.

Wide swaths of this book were written or revised at the Vermont Studio Center, the Virginia Center for the Creative Arts, in the Lower Manhattan Cultural Council's Workspace Residency, and in The Poetry Project's Emerge-Surface-Be fellowship. Thank you to these institutions for their support.

Special thanks to Anselm Berrigan and Stacy Szymaszek for their mentorship both through and outside of The Poetry Project; Carmen Giménez Smith for more than a decade of guidance; Belladonna* Collaborative and its members for giving me a sense of purpose during a long wayward period; Emily Skillings for art direction and savvy; and Christine Shan Shan Hou for use of her collage *Self-actualization (forward movement)*.

Krystal Languell lives in Chicago. Her previous books are *Call the Catastrophists* (BlazeVox, 2011) and *Gray Market* (1913 Press, 2016). She has also published six chapbooks, including *Be a Dead Girl* (Argos Books, 2014) and *Archive Theft*, a collection of interviews, (Essay Press, 2015). A NYSCA/NYFA 2017 Artist Fellowship Finalist in Poetry, she has also completed a 2014–15 Lower Manhattan Cultural Council workspace residency and a 2013–14 Poetry Project Emerge-Surface-Be fellowship. Since 2010, she has helped coordinate the activities of Belladonna* Collaborative while publishing the feminist poetry journal *Bone Bouquet*. She was an adjunct in New York City for seven years.